ECO JOURNEYs

LIFE OF A GLASS JAR

by Louise Nelson

BEARPORT
PUBLISHING

Minneapolis, Minnesota

Credits

Front cover – grafvision, Monkey Business Images, kim chul hyun. 3 – DioGen/Shutterstock, Matt Benoit/Shutterstock, phichit Bhumadhana/Shutterstock. 4 – pilipphoto/Shutterstock. 4&5 – Tekkol, Kichigin. 6&7 – Ivaschenko Roman, DyziO. 8&9 – Africa Studio, dugwy39. 10&11 – vchal, mountainpix. 12&13 – Fotografiche, Evan Lorne. 14&15 – Photographee.eu, AVAVA, TeeStocker, Phovoir, rodimov. 16&17 – Somnuek saelim, Anton Kurashenko. 18 – Marek Trawczynski/iStock. 18&19 – Nataliia Yankovets, Atiketta Sangasaeng, ryby, roundex, Alter-ego, Somboon Bunproy, krasky, Africa Studio. 20 – Smiltena/Shutterstock. 20&21 – Olga Madlewska, HollyHarry, Sharomka, Akhmad Dody Firmansyah, photosync. 22&23 – KAMPIAN CHENRAM, Andrii Spy_k, myboys.me, yalayama, Benoit Daoust. 24 – Floortje/iStock. Images are courtesy of Shutterstock.com. With thanks to Getty Images, Thinkstock Photo, and iStockphoto.

Library of Congress Cataloging-in-Publication Data

Names: Nelson, Louise, author.
Title: Life of a glass jar / by Louise Nelson.
Description: Fusion books. | Minneapolis, Minnesota : Bearport Publishing Company, [2023] | Series: Eco journey | Includes index.
Identifiers: LCCN 2021061529 (print) | LCCN 2021061530 (ebook) | ISBN 9781636918990 (library binding) | ISBN 9781636919041 (paperback) | ISBN 9781636919096 (ebook)
Subjects: LCSH: Glass waste--Recycling--Juvenile literature. | Glass jars--Recycling--Juvenile literature. | Recycling (Waste, etc.)--Juvenile literature. | Recycled products--Juvenile literature.
Classification: LCC TP859.7 .N45 2023 (print) | LCC TP859.7 (ebook) | DDC 666/.19--dc23/eng/20211230
LC record available at https://lccn.loc.gov/2021061529
LC ebook record available at https://lccn.loc.gov/2021061530

For more information, write to Bearport Publishing, 5357 Penn Avenue South, Minneapolis, MN 55419. Printed in the United States of America.

Contents

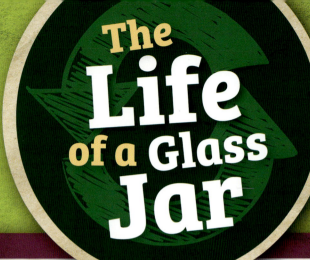

The Life of a Glass Jar

Glass jars are useful **containers**. They are often used to hold food. You have probably seen jars of jam at the store.

When glass jars are empty, they can be washed and used again. Jars can be **reused** in this way for a long time.

Do you know what happens to a glass jar when you're done using it?

What Is Glass?

Glass is hard and smooth. It is often clear and shiny.

Glass jars have lids to keep things inside. The lids are often made of metal.

6

Glass is made from sand. The sand is heated until it **melts**. Then, it can be shaped into different objects, such as jars.

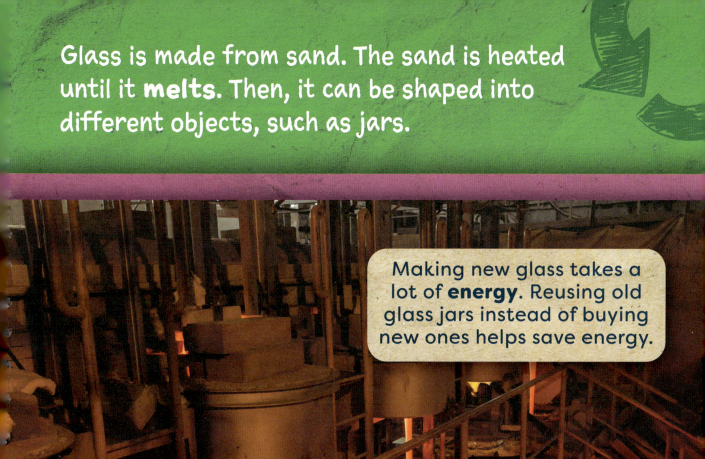

Making new glass takes a lot of **energy**. Reusing old glass jars instead of buying new ones helps save energy.

Used Again *and* Again

A glass jar can be reused again and again. But glass can break if it is dropped. Then, you can no longer use it.

Broken glass is sharp. Never touch it. Always get an adult.

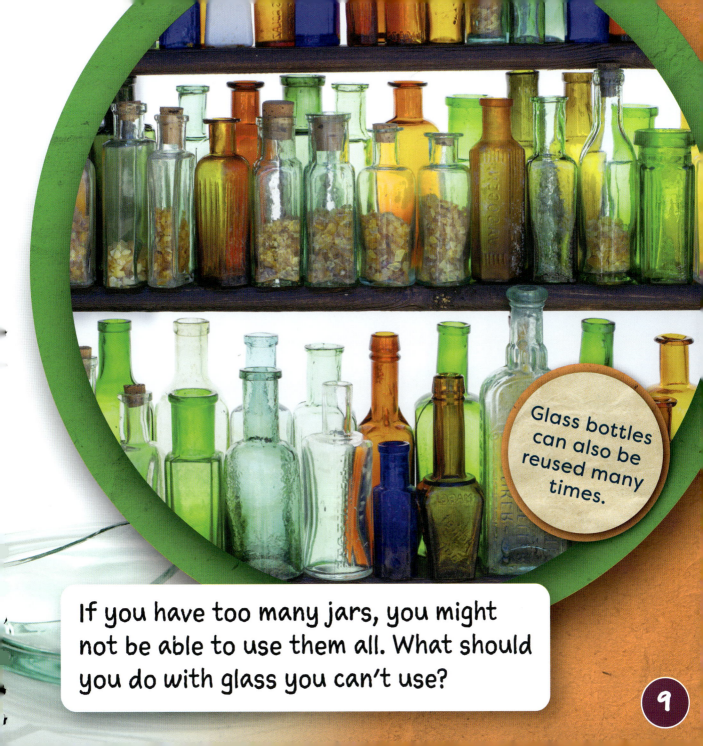

Glass bottles can also be reused many times.

If you have too many jars, you might not be able to use them all. What should you do with glass you can't use?

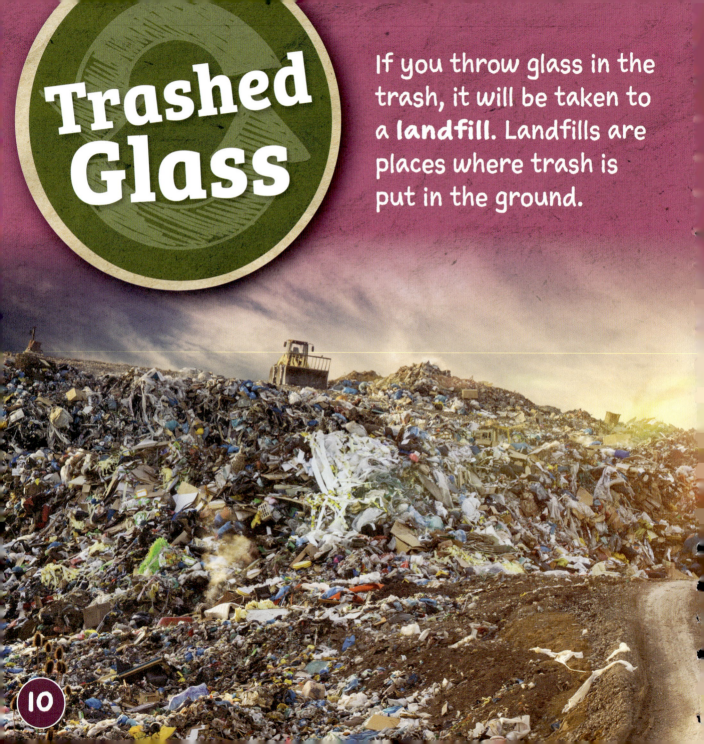

Trashed Glass

If you throw glass in the trash, it will be taken to a **landfill**. Landfills are places where trash is put in the ground.

Some trash breaks down quickly and becomes dirt. But glass stays in landfills for a very long time. When trash doesn't break down, it **pollutes** the land.

This glass vase was made thousands of years ago. The glass still has not broken down.

What Is Recycling?

When trash builds up in landfills, it harms Earth. But some things don't need to be thrown in the trash. Glass, paper, plastic, and metal can be **recycled** instead.

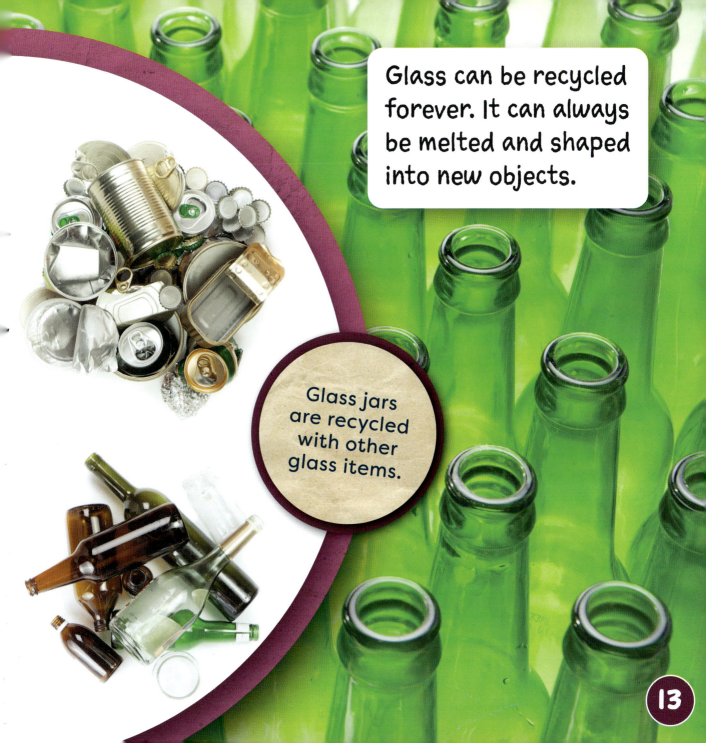

Glass can be recycled forever. It can always be melted and shaped into new objects.

Glass jars are recycled with other glass items.

Recycling a Glass Jar

Before you recycle a glass jar, you should wash it. Take off the label and lid, too.

Metal and plastic lids can also be recycled.

14

When the jar is clean, put it in a recycling bin. Everything in the bin will be taken to a recycling center.

Where can you find a recycling bin?

At home

At school

In parks and other **public** places

Sort, Smash, and Melt

At the recycling center, glass is **sorted** by type and color. Then, it is smashed into tiny pieces called cullet.

This cullet is ready to be made into new glass.

The cullet is taken to a factory. Then, the factory melts it to make new glass.

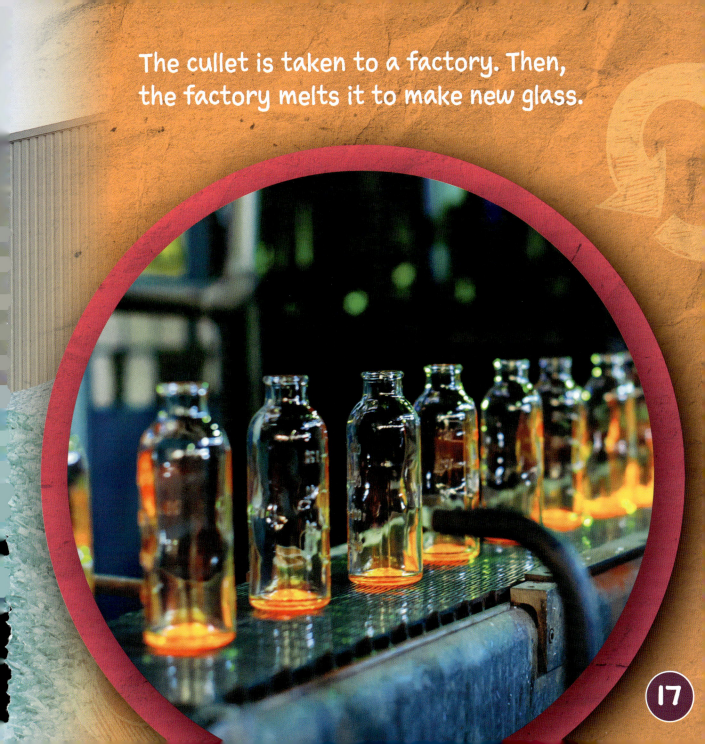

Trash to Treasure

When a glass jar is recycled, it can become part of a new glass object. Here are some things that can be made from recycled glass . . .

A glass cup

A glass lampshade

Marbles

Glass beads

A new jar

Most glass objects have some recycled glass in them.

A glass vase

19

Reuse and Upcycle

Recycling helps Earth. But you can also help by reusing jars at home!

Old jars can hold many things, including school supplies.

One way to reuse glass jars is to upcycle them. Upcycling means making something old into something else. What could you make?

A lantern

A bank

A toothbrush holder

A snow globe

21

The Eco Journey of a Glass Jar

The glass is turned into something new.

The jar is sorted and melted with other glass.

The jar is bought and used.

When it is empty, the jar is washed.

The jar is thrown in a recycling bin and taken to a recycling center.

22

Quick Quiz

Can you remember the eco journey of a glass jar? Let's see! Look back through the book if you can't remember.

1. What is glass made from?
a) Sand
b) Fabric
c) Aluminum

2. What is crushed glass ready for recycling called?
a) Crumpet
b) Cullet
c) Custard

3. How many times can glass be recycled?
a) Once
b) Ten times
c) Again and again, forever

4. What should you do before recycling a glass jar?
a) Break the jar
b) Wash the jar
c) Throw the jar away

Answers: 1) a, 2) b, 3) c, 4) b

Glossary

containers things that other things can be put in

energy power used to make something work or happen

landfill a large hole in the ground used for dumping garbage

melts turns to liquid because of heat

pollutes makes things dirty in a way that harms Earth

public open to all people in the community

recycled collected, sorted, and made into new materials

reused used again

sorted put into groups

Index

24